YouCue Feelings:
Using Online Videos for Social Learning

Anna Vagin, PhD

Copyright © 2015 Ann Vagin, PhD

All rights reserved.

ISBN:
ISBN-13: 978-1507654941
ISBN-10: 1507654944

DEDICATION

For Carly and Jake, who give me a reason to work hard and an opportunity to show what a gift it is to love your work.

"If your emotional abilities aren't in hand, if you don't have self-awareness, if you are not able to manage distressing emotions, if you can't have empathy and have effective relationships, then no matter how smart you are, you are not going to get very far."
—Daniel Goleman, *Emotional Intelligence* (2005)

CONTENTS

	Acknowledgments	i
1	Introducing YouCue Feelings	3
2	Getting Ready	11
3	YouTube Video Summaries & Links	25
4	YouCue Activities	33
5	Moving Ahead	59
	Appendix A	63
	Appendix B	65
	Appendix C	71
	Appendix D	79
	Appendix E	81
	Bibliography	83

ACKNOWLEDGMENTS

Thank you to the families and students I learn from daily.

Thank you to the YouTube™ video community for wonderful stories, animation, and the willingness of so many animators to share their work.

Thank you to my "team": Elana Dolberg, my wise organizer and encourager-in-chief, Sandy Horwich, editor extraordinaire, Stephen Noetzel, master of layout, and Alison Brown, cover designer.

Always, thank you to my husband Bruce, and my children Carly and Jake, for whom I make too few desserts. And my kind, sweet, hard working Dad. I love you all!

Chapter 1

Introducing YouCue Feelings

There's nothing like an engaging story. Whether it's a familiar book, a stirring movie, or an amusing tale we ask a beloved grandparent to retell time and time again, stories can both entertain and instruct. In spoken words, pictures, gestures, animation, or film, stories show us the human experience. YouCue Feelings uses a relatively new form of storytelling—YouTube videos—as material for learning about relationships.

The Program

YouCue Feelings (YCF) is a program for elementary and middle school age students who struggle with social understanding (often as an outcome of Autism Spectrum, ADD/ADHD, or other diagnoses). Created for therapists, teachers, and parents for use in individual, small group, classroom, and home environments, YCF contains links to preselected YouTube videos as well as activities (called YouCues) specifically created to build children's social knowledge. For younger students, YCF incorporates storybooks (either ones you already have or choose from a suggested list) to reinforce learning. Typically-developing students can also benefit; YCF provides opportunities for them to practice what they already know.

The videos and activities in YCF have been carefully chosen to engage students, jump start learning, and focus discussions about a range of fundamental social learning concepts. Watching creatively rendered stories followed by easy activities makes YCF an appealing and effective tool. Students may not even realize that they're building crucial skills. YouCue activities range from simple drawing projects or discussions about the characters in a YouTube video, to more sophisticated activities such as building connections between the social learning concepts in videos and what happens in a student's everyday life.

Our goal for students with social learning challenges is for them to acquire social relationship skills that will improve their capacity for effective, fulfilling relationships with family members, people at their school or work, and members of their broader community. This is a large and complicated task. YouCue Feelings simplifies such learning (Graphic 1).

Graphic 1. The components of YouCue Feelings

This book contains everything you need to start using YouTube videos as social learning material. *The focus of this book is feelings because emotions are fundamental to relationships and social interactions.* It will help students develop their ability to label feelings and track feelings changing over time (Illustration 1), as well as talk about their own emotional experiences. Countless YouTube videos portray feelings, and this book introduces you to 25 great choices.

Become familiar with the videos, review the activities, and gather the suggested materials (see Chapter 2). Then you'll be ready to fire up your Internet connection and start YouCue Feelings!

Illustration 1. Student illustration of an uncomfortable feeling in a Minecraft YouTube video.

Illustration 2. Student illustration of a comfortable feeling in a Minecraft YouTube video.

YouCue Feelings is the first of a series. Upcoming YouCue materials will:

- Present new sets of preselected YouTube videos and YouCue activities to cover:
    a. Internal processes: flexibility, perseverance, and perspective taking
    b. Relationship processes: cooperation, helping, jerky behavior, bumps in relationships, repairs, and "re-dos"

- Update the YouCue feelings list of recommended YouTube videos
- Expand the already released sets of YouCue activities
- Supply templates for writing social learning goals and measuring progress

Register your purchase at www.socialtime.org *to receive free updates. Also, check the website to learn about additional materials.*

The Importance of Social Learning

Social interaction surrounds us as we move through our lives. Even when we aren't actively engaged in interaction, we're still exposed to it—we can see and hear it. Social exposure provides us with critical information that guides our social learning. From our observations and experiences we learn what does and doesn't work. We learn how to repair our social errors. We apply what we've picked up over time as we continue to learn what is and isn't effective.

Of course, not all of us have the same degree of interest in or ability to process the social information that surrounds us (Lipton & Nowicki, 2009; Baron-Cohen, 1995). Some of us, from a very early age, are facile at interpreting the feeling states of others, engaging easily with those around us. Others struggle to interpret the confusing code of social engagement. Individual "wiring," among other factors, results in varying levels of social ability.

In the past decade, many materials have been developed for students who struggle to understand, develop, and maintain social relationships. The YCF program is meant to be one tool in your social teaching toolbox. *This program assumes a working knowledge of the communicative and interpersonal issues of students with challenges in social cognition.* If you're just getting started in this area, a great place to find a lot of relevant information is Michelle Garcia Winner's Social Thinking® website: www.socialthinking.com.

Feelings First

You may be wondering why YouCue begins with feelings. After all, there are many social "behaviors" we want our students using—or not using! There's so much for them to learn about the dance of social interaction. Well, feelings form a base for all of that (Tomkins, 2008; Ekman, 2007).

At the heart of relationships is the ability to discern how others are feeling as well as what they're thinking and planning. To identify the feelings of others, we need an emotional vocabulary beyond "happy," "sad," and "mad." More sophisticated emotional vocabulary is everywhere, from books to TV shows to talk around the Thanksgiving table. This vocabulary often describes gradations of feelings. For example, "annoyed" is a smaller-sized feeling, and "furious" is a larger-sized feeling in the feeling family "angry." We need to understand gradations of feelings so that our interactions match the situation. *Do your students resist talking about "feeling words"? Show them a cool YouTube and see how many they come up with* (Illustration 3).

comfortable	uncomfortable
happy	annoyed
OK	mad
excited	furious
silly	grouchy
pleased	upset
successful	frustrated
surprised	explosive
	sad
	upset

Illustration 3. Feelings list developed by a class of fourth graders after watching a YouTube video. Nice!

To be socially successful, we need to interact differently with someone who is annoyed than with someone who is furious. The child who has difficulty noticing these gradations, or perhaps even labeling basic emotions, may not recognize a peer is angry until that person is *very* angry. Oops, too late!

Students with social-cognitive challenges may also find it hard to identify and differentiate the size of their own feelings. This skill is important because the more we know about feelings, the better we are at dealing with uncomfortable emotions (Barret, et al., 2001; Bloom, 1998), and the better our social interactions are in general.

If we can catch ourselves before we get too upset, we have a greater chance of making a change that helps us feel better. If we wait too long, we may be overwhelmed by uncomfortable feelings, making it more challenging to figure out and implement solutions. Many students with social learning challenges experience a lot of *big* feelings.

They become very angry or very sad. Because they're unaware of or misinterpret more subtle feelings, their emotional development is limited.

Feelings are always in transition, rarely remaining in one state for long. Understanding and tolerating these shifts, as well as developing tools for managing them, is fundamental to our social success. YouCue Feelings encourages students to learn about feelings with motivating and enjoyable materials.

The Crucial Role of Context

Of course, feelings don't happen in a vacuum. Feelings and context are complementary; neither occurs without the other. Feelings arise as we interact with the world, within dynamic contexts that are constantly shifting and never exactly the same. *Students with social learning difficulties struggle to figure out and keep up with what contextual cues are socially relevant* (Vermeulen, 2012).

To fit with those around us (and figure out what others are thinking), we must constantly scan and process contextual information to determine what's happening as well as what we need to be doing and not doing. Being socially observant of context involves determining not just what others are thinking about but their intentions as well as feelings. As people act to achieve their intended goal through execution of a plan, they affect those around them, their feelings as well as actions. It gets very complicated, yet this web of contextual processing is what leads us to understand what's expected of us and how we can achieve what we want.

The better we are at figuring out what others are thinking, planning, and feeling, the more successful we'll probably be in our attempts at interaction. People communicate much of this information using channels that can be tricky for our students to figure out: fleeting eye gaze, facial expression, nonverbal movement, and tone of voice.

Constantly monitoring contextual changes to make sure we're doing what's expected and acceptable is critical. Our most successful social interactions take place when our contextual processing skills and emotional awareness allow us to take care of our own as well as the other person's feelings.

In my previous book, *Movie Time Social Learning* (2012), I presented a structured format for building these skills using popular movies.

Though YCF activities don't focus on these fundamental skills (e.g., contextual processing to determine socially relevant information) directly, please remember their importance, and discuss thoughts and plans of characters in context. *Sticky notes presenting thoughts and plans on a paused frame placed above characters' heads can reinforce what students are figuring out.*

YouTube as Social Learning Material

Current research suggests that students on the Autism Spectrum struggle with the processing of social motion—how our movements provide information about our intent (Kroeger, et al., 2013; Kaiser & Pelphrey, 2012; Klin et al., 2009). For example, let's say I'm building a PlayDoh snowman and someone takes its head off and smushes it. I gather my materials and move to another table looking upset. My intent could be interpreted (based on contextual cues and social knowledge) as "she's upset and is going to build it again away from the person who smushed it." However, a student with social challenges would probably give a more limited interpretation based solely on concrete action: "She's moving her stuff to another table." If you don't realize the important pieces of information of *smushed snowman* (concrete fact) and *upset because I liked it the way I was building it* (intuiting how my feeling relates to my plan and how my plan was derailed by the actions of someone), you're less likely to spontaneously express empathy or tell the smusher to stop messing with other people's PlayDoh. Or, if you're the smusher, you may not realize that anything is wrong at all or snap at those who try to point out your error.

Students with social learning challenges have a harder time scanning context for relevant social details, following plans of people, and incorporating nonverbal information into their social understanding. One crucial element in improving such skills is exposure and guided teaching (Ukrainetz, 1998). YCF provides the opportunity for contextualized guided teaching with online videos and storybooks.

Life as we experience it can't be replayed. But media (movies, movie shorts, and YouTube videos) can be paused, rewound, and studied as interactions and events unfold (Suskind, 2014). Watching media in structured ways allows students to practice social attention. We all find it challenging to look at our own behavior. When building social understanding, it's "much easier, as well as far more enjoyable, to identify and label the mistakes of others than to recognize our own" (Kahneman, 2011). Talking about the uncomfortable feelings, mistakes, and successes of others can make it easier for us to admit that we face similar situations, recognizing that we all sometimes stumble, sometimes feel uncomfortable, and sometimes succeed.

YCF uses the appealing story lines of short, easily accessed videos as engaging and relationship-rich teaching material. YouTube videos selected for YCF have great story lines, full of emotions and interpersonal engagement. Most students are more than happy to watch a YouTube video and then talk about their observations. *When chosen carefully, there's something for everyone on YouTube.* YouCue Feelings makes it easy to guide students in thinking about, talking about, and ultimately, practicing important social learning ideas in their everyday lives.

Coming Up

Upcoming chapters will give you all the information you need to use YouCue Feelings.

- **Chapter 2:** Getting Ready…This chapter acquaints you with the program.
- **Chapter 3:** YouTube Video Summaries & Links…Find information about the preselected online videos here.
- **Chapter 4:** YouCue Activities…This chapter contains 50 activities to build emotional understanding.
- **Chapter 5:** Moving Ahead…Find information about expanding YCF with your own ideas.
- **Appendix…** Appendices are important! Here you'll find video and YouCue pairing guides, suggested books, materials, and lists to support emotional learning, and additional information.

Ready to keep going? Your next stop is Chapter 2.

Chapter 2

Getting Ready

Before using YouCue Feelings with students, you need to be familiar with the contents of the program. This chapter will answer questions such as:

How do I select students for YCF? In what learning environments can YCF be used? See "Selecting Students" below.

How do I get started? See "Equipment and Materials,", "Setting Up for Success" and "First Steps" in this chapter.

Is there a particular order I need to follow? See "First Steps" and "Suggested Sequences" in this chapter.

How do I know students are doing the work correctly? See "First Steps" in this chapter and student work examples throughout this book.

I've looked at some of the YouTube videos, and there's such a range of stories. Some seem pretty mature. I teach a third grade class! Keep in mind that YouCue Feelings can be used with students from kindergarten through eighth grade. Not all videos are appropriate for all students. See "Where Do I Start?" in this chapter.

In Chapter 1, you mentioned books. I thought YCF was about videos? You will be using books with younger students. See "A Word About Books" in this chapter.

I'm a parent. Can I use YCF at home? Yes, see "A Word for Parents" in this chapter.

Selecting Students

Students who can benefit from YouCue Feelings include children with:
- A range of identified diagnoses: Autism Spectrum Disorder, Social (Pragmatic) Communication Disorder, ADHD, or Nonverbal Learning Disability
- Verbal language but limited emotional vocabulary and narrative skills who struggle with perspective taking and have difficulties understanding the unspoken rules of social interaction
- No specific diagnosis but who struggle with social relationships
- Typical development. *Elementary school is a time of social learning for everyone.*

As mentioned in Chapter 1, YCF can be used in many settings:
- With kindergarten through eighth grade students
- In classrooms, small groups, or individually
- During therapeutic sessions (speech and language, counseling, and psychotherapy)
- In home schools as part of the social curriculum
- At home as a family

YouTube Video Summaries

This book includes summaries and links to 25 carefully selected YouTube videos that portray a range of feelings really well. Because your first step is to choose what videos you want to show students, use these summaries, which also show the length of each segment, to get ideas about where to start. The videos are listed in a suggested developmental order for viewing. Because YouCue Feelings includes a wide range of recommended YouTube videos to fit a wide range of student ages, read and/or preview an assortment so you can select material that's most appropriate for your students. A number of videos can be used to work on expressive language and narrative, important aspects of social understanding.

Your students will watch the videos before doing the YouCue activities. Level 1 YouCues work directly with the videos. For Level 2 YouCues, the videos serve as warm up. You can use one video for multiple YouCues or mix things up and watch different videos. You don't want material to get stale, so showing different videos helps students stay engaged. Appendix A includes links to view two spreadsheets that will help you pair videos and YouCue activities.

YouCues

YouCue activities are the core of YouCue Feelings. YouCues introduce targeted social concepts and present a step-by-step approach to building understanding. Working with videos first allows students to examine and discuss the feelings and social behavior of others before they look and talk about what *they* themselves feel and do (and what they may be doing "wrong" or what adults want them to change).

None of us enjoys being asked to look at our weaknesses or to do things that are particularly difficult. Students with social thinking issues are no different. *By starting with engaging characters, students can build their social knowledge and their comfort level with discussions about social relationships.* Later, they'll be more ready and willing to think about themselves, even when that leads to uncomfortable feelings.

Learning comes from multiple examples. YouCue Feelings emphasizes that students need to view and discuss multiple examples of each idea to really understand important yet complicated social concepts. One YouTube video can't display all the permutations and complexities of feelings such as "frustrated" or "worried." It's easier for students to generalize to *their world* (in which contexts are always different) if they've seen many different contextual examples from the *video world*.

YouCue activities include drawing, making lists, and discussing impressions. There are two levels of YouCue activities. Level 1 uses YouTube videos (and books for students through fourth grade) as social learning material. Level 2 uses personal observations, first of others we know and then of ourselves. Level 2 activities include ideas to connect what students have learned to real-time situations. It's a good idea to go through the YouCues in order because later activities often call on work products from earlier YouCues.

Because it's important for students to work with the feelings of characters before moving on to discussions about their own experiences, I suggest that you work quite a few Level 1 YouCues before moving on to Level 2 (Graphic 2).

	Minimum number of YouCue activities completed with online videos	Minimum number of YouCue activities completed with books
Kindergarten through 4th grade	5	5
5th through 8th grade	8	N/A

Graphic 2. Recommended Number of Level 1 YouCues Completed Before Moving to Level 2 YouCues

Note: *At any time, if students bring up their own experiences, even with activities that focus on characters, encourage discussion.* That's ultimately what we want them to do—draw connections between what they see on-screen and what they themselves experience.

After you've followed the age-appropriate sequence with Level 1, you and your students are ready to move on to Level 2. Though these activities focus on discussions about students themselves or others they know, there are suggested YouTube videos you can use to set the stage (Appendix A-2). At this level, give students a broad experience by having them complete at least ten Level 2 YouCues. Take your time and enjoy the journey.

Level 2 YouCues emphasize student observations of others and themselves. As you support students in looking at their own behavior and feelings, make sure to work slowly and gently. It's better to take your time and allow for self-reflection than to rush through to complete the activity. Remember, this work can feel novel and therefore threatening. Going over YouCues more than once can lead to deeper understanding (Illustration 4). New ideas and realizations don't happen overnight.

> They were escorting me at recess and lunch because I was impulsive and lost patience with other kids. My behavior had been mean (like pulling sweatshirts and saying mean things).
> I also asked kids if they ever talked about suicide. That made kids feel shocked and scared and disturbed.
> I didn't always do this stuff, just sometimes.

Illustration 4. Student work: Self-Reflection #1, Level 2 YouCue

As you work with the videos, feel free to stop and rewind as needed to support student understanding. A great freeze-frame of an expression can give students that extra information to come up with a great answer. Go slowly and let the story sink in. *Remember, processing time of students with social learning challenges may be long—viewing them multiple times often leads to greater learning. Build understanding over time.*

As you use Level 1 and 2 YouCues with YouTube videos, you may find that many other relevant social cognitive issues arise. Their richness is one of the great things about these videos. While more YouCues are being developed covering ideas such as cooperation, repairing bumps in relationships, dealing with "jerky" behavior, etc., feel free to ad lib your own YouCues in these other important directions.

A Word About Books

As mentioned above, students in grades K–4 will be using books to supplement their emotional learning with videos. For these younger students, well-chosen books are wonderful teaching tools. Generalized learning comes from reviewing material in different ways. Using storybooks with your students allows them to study feelings of characters using materials that they can hold, independently examine, and easily share with those around them.

You'll use the content of books in the same way as the videos. You can use one story for multiple YouCues or use different stories for each activity. The most important thing is to keep your students interested! Choose books from your own collection or from the library that focus on feelings. Appendix B lists some of my favorites—

which are readily available in most libraries—along with brief descriptions.

Equipment and Materials

To use YouCue Feelings, you need access to YouTube through an Internet connection on a computer or tablet. Because you'll show videos to your students, it's best to have as large a screen as possible for viewing—it's hard to fit four students around a smart phone. *It's crucial to preview the YouTube videos so you know the story and how you'll use the accompanying activities.*

Be aware that YouTube often shows commercials before a video begins. Some you can skip after several seconds, but some require that you watch the whole thing. Cue up before students enter, especially because the commercials aren't something you want students seeing anyway (many commercials are *not* kid-appropriate). You may want to experiment with downloading videos or using commercial-blocking apps. Consult your local teen (or kindergarten student!).

Practice going full screen and pausing the video. Timing is everything. Gather supporting materials so your teaching flows smoothly. Remember that students with social learning challenges often do best with visual supports. Writing down or making quick sketches can help students keep the social information you're discussing in working memory.

Dry-erase boards and markers are essential—you can never have too many. Some activities involve student drawing, so make sure to have enough for everyone. Dry-erase boards are easier to erase than paper and pencils or crayons and so are more fun. They're also exceptionally useful for recording information during group discussions. Get an assortment of sizes if you can. When you create a great work product with students, snap a quick photo so you can use that information later.

Sticky notes can also be very helpful. Use them to record information (character thoughts, feelings, and plans), and place them directly on a paused screen.

You'll also need visual supports for feelings vocabulary (see Appendix C for options). It's easier to expand emotional vocabulary when you have sets of pictures or lists of emotions so that students can experiment with options.

In summary, here's what you should gather:

- ✓ This YouCue Feelings book
- ✓ Internet connection
- ✓ Dry erase boards
- ✓ Sticky notes
- ✓ Visual supports

Setting Up for Success

Now that you have your materials organized, what about the students? How can you set up your sessions to be most effective? Here are some tips based on my own experiments using YCF:

Groups of three to four students work best. If you have a larger group, be sure your screen is big enough for all to see. You want to view all together.

Individual work lets you focus on exactly the needs of that student. While very different from group work, it can be equally productive.

With younger students I usually work for about 20 minutes and a bit longer with older students. Of course, if you're on a roll, stay with it.

I suggest viewing just one video or reading just one book per session and pairing it with one or two YouCues. Reviewing YouCue work usually leads to productive discussion.

YCF works well as a "break" after other focused work. The viewing or reading and drawing activities let students relax, regroup, and re-regulate.

First Steps

This book provides quite a few suggested YouTube videos and YouCues. You may be wondering what to do first with all these videos and levels and activities (and second, and third…). This section gives that information.

YCF doesn't give you worksheets to copy, follow, and fill out. There aren't sequences that tell you exactly what to do. That's because all students are different, with varying levels of emotional knowledge and different needs. The information you get from students is individual to them, and you're the one to decide what online videos and YouCues to use. Here are some suggested steps to become familiar with the materials and be able to tailor them for your students.

Step 1. Your first choice will be deciding what YouTube video(s) you want to work with. Read the summaries and watch some of the listed YouTube videos. You'll like some while finding others less interesting. That's okay. Only use the ones you like.

Step 2. As you watch, think about the students with whom you work. Which students would like which videos?

Step 3. Now, think about what your students know about feelings. Start paying attention to their emotional knowledge. Can they label "mad," "sad," and "happy," or do they have a tendency to say "feels good" and "feels bad" when you ask for a feeling label? If you ask students to be more specific, can they come up with appropriate and more sophisticated vocabulary, such as "frustrated" or "nervous," or are they still at "mad" and "sad"? How do students handle their own uncomfortable feelings and even those of others? Get ready to experiment.

Step 4. Dive in! Choose a student or group of students, select a YouTube video for them, and start with Level 1. Follow the guidance in The Big Idea and Help It Happen, and look over the Level 1 YouCues. The first one is always a good place to start. It will get you talking, drawing, and thinking about feelings with students. Try it and see what happens (Illustration 5).

> Ormie wanted to get the cookies but they were too high!
>
> | comfortable | uncomfortable |
> |---|---|
> | excited | mad |
> | happy | disappointed |
> | | hurt |
> | | sad |

Illustration 5. Student work on Day #1 using Ormie the Pig. Naming Feelings and Comfortable vs. Uncomfortable Feelings YouCues.

Step 5. Think about and choose a natural progression in activities. What do you think these students would like to do next? Do you want to move to the next YouCue, or should they re-work the activity with another video? What do you think they should learn about next? What would keep them engaged? You can use new videos or stay with a favorite. Try a YouCue with a book for younger students one day, a video the next. It's important to mix things up to keep it fun.

Step 6. Keep track of what videos, books, and YouCues you use. Take quick photos of student work. If you have more questions, check my website (www.socialtime.org) for information or email me directly. YCF is a program that welcomes communication and ideas.

Suggested Sequences

Let's take a look at some sequences you may want to use when you work with YouCue Feelings. You want to develop a sense of the many videos and activities and combine them in ways that work for you. These are just suggestions.

Option 1. Level 1 only: Good for everyone but especially younger students

For students who need to build up their emotional vocabulary and may not be ready yet to talk about their own experiences, you can focus on Level 1. Watch many different YouTube videos and read a wide range of books (with K–4th graders) as you deepen their comfort level with and understanding of feelings. A simple yet effective plan can be to work with one video or book each session or week, making this a unit on feeling words. You're doing important work by talking about feelings with fun materials. Students may not even realize how much they're learning. At some point, you'll judge them ready to explore Level 2 YouCues.

Option 2. Level 1 leading to Level 2: Good for students who are ready for more

Begin the program with some YouTube videos (and books with younger students), and go through YouCues in Level 1. When you're ready and have completed the recommended number (refer to Graphic 2 earlier in this chapter), move to Level 2 YouCues. As you move into Level 2, you can re-watch favorite videos used in Level 1 or use new ones for variety.

Option 3. Levels 1 and 2 together: The full treatment!

Follow Option 2, but once you enter Level 2 YouCues, continue to work on Level 1 YouCues with new videos and books. You can switch between the two levels depending on what your students enjoy. You may come up with more activities on your own—fantastic!

As new YouCue materials become available, you'll be able to add new videos as well as new YouCues to your repertoire. (Remember to register your purchase at www.socialtime.org to receive free updates.)

Sample YouCue Work Examples

YouCues help you structure activities with students. However, because every child or group of children is unique, you have a lot of discretion as to how you implement the actual work.

The more you experiment with YouCue Feelings, the more sure of yourself you'll become. You'll feel confident with following where the group discussion leads, while keeping in mind your goals and reasons for watching any particular video. You'll feel more comfortable generating visual supports of your own as well as supporting students in creating their own images. Also, you'll get to know the suggested videos, and matching them to students will become much easier.

To help you get an idea of what student work products *might* look like, scattered throughout this book (mostly in Chapter 4) are examples of work produced by students. Take a look at these, but remember, the work produced by *your* students will look *original to them*. They'll learn best by showing you what they know, think, and feel (Illustration 6). Your job will be to take them further in their emotional and social understanding. Sometimes it will be baby steps, at other times larger leaps.

Illustration 6.
Student example:
Self-Sketching #2
Level 2 YouCue.

A Word of Caution

As you begin to use YCF with students, you may find them eager to share what they think are "great" YouTube videos with you and other students. *Don't show any YouTube video without personally previewing it first by yourself.* Many videos that start off well may surprise you a few seconds later. Again, be on the lookout for commercials. They're prevalent and often target adult audiences. No remote is powerful enough to rewind and undo the viewing of an inappropriate word or image.

Communicating with Your Team

Watching YouTube for social learning may be a new concept for you and your students, and for parents, teachers, and administrators as well. Before you start YouCue Feelings, educate your team so they understand *why* you're letting students watch YouTube.

You can use the sample letter from Appendix E, or spend some time with them discussing how YouTube videos can help students understand crucial social learning concepts that underlie core curriculum. Remember, it's better to cover your bases first and thereby avoid getting calls asking "Why is my student watching YouTube when she's supposed to be working?"

A Note Before You Dive In

Each learning community has its own opinions of what's appropriate for students of a particular age to watch, as does every family.

The videos suggested in YCF are suggestions. Please use your good judgment when deciding what videos to show. Always err on the side of caution. It's your responsibility to make YouCue Feelings a positive experience for all.

The YouTube videos recommended in YCF are available at the time of publication. However, it's possible that a video may "disappear" from YouTube—that's part of the YouTube platform. I do my best to monitor the availability of videos and will release updated lists of recommended YouTube videos from time to time. These updates will be available to those who have purchased YCF materials and have registered their purchase.

A Word for Parents

YouCue Feelings works well for families. Whether you're watching alone with your child or enjoying videos with siblings, YouCue activities can be a family project. However, here are some caveats:

Children work differently with parents than with other adults. You may come out ahead if you lead by example. When a YouCue suggests drawing, you can draw your own example whether your child does or not. Show him or her your sketch and talk about it. If your child makes comments, feel free to start a conversation. Keep things light. Children will learn just by looking at your examples.

Expressing uncertainty on your part can be an effective ploy: "I'm not sure, do you think he felt sad or mad?" or "It's kind of tricky to figure this out..." Children feel less pressure when they don't think we have all the answers and will be more willing to take a risk.

Engage siblings, but contain their exuberance. Brothers and sisters may have great language skills and may be quick to label emotions and explain their own examples. If this is the case in your home, you may want to take turns with ideas or start YouCue Feelings at times when siblings aren't around.

You have home court advantage. You can talk about the videos you've watched and books you've read in the car, at the dinner table, when visiting Grandma, etc. Use the YCF program as a springboard for more conversations about feelings.

Have Faith in Your Own Skills

Every social learning experience is different. Students have different needs and interests. You may have time limitations or want to follow relevant discussions where they lead. My belief is that there are few, if any, rigid rules in social learning work. You need to use your judgment to determine what social learning concepts are most needed by your students, when students may need more discussion, and when they're ready to move on. Those are decisions you need to make yourself, and the more you challenge yourself to make them, the more successful you'll find your work.

Ready to keep going? Start checking out some of the recommended YouTube videos as you read their descriptions in Chapter 3. And, if you haven't already done so, register your purchase of YCF with www.socialtime.org.

Chapter 3

YouTube Video Summaries & Links

These summaries are presented in a *suggested* developmental sequence. The earlier videos are great for all ages. Some of the videos listed later are for slightly older students. You need to judge what will work for your students. Read these summaries, preview, and choose carefully. I've listed the exact title and link of each YouTube video as of the time of this printing. If the video doesn't appear when you enter the title in your YouTube search, try typing the link and see if the video appears that matches the description. Appendix A contains links to view two spreadsheets detailing which videos are particularly well suited to specific activities. Enjoy!

(1) Ormie the Pig (Arc Productions, Oct. 31, 2011)

https://www.youtube.com/watch?v=EUm-vAOmV1o

In this four-minute video, Ormie tries hard to get some cookies off the top of the refrigerator. He's ingenious and comes up with many ideas, none of which works until the very end. His many feelings during the course of this video and the surprise ending can spark interesting discussion and social guessing about what will happen next.

(2) Classic Sesame Street—Ernie Counts Fruit (Sesame Street, Jan. 31, 2007)

https://www.youtube.com/watch?v=6bz_FQA8jjk

In this two-and-a-half-minute classic Sesame Street clip, Bert becomes frustrated with Ernie as he counts his fruit. This excellent video depicts the frustrations that come up when friends don't listen to what we're trying to tell them and don't pay attention to how we're feeling. Although Bert experiences some strong feelings, he's able to stay calm and patient—a great example of coping with frustration.

(3) A Cloudy Lesson by Yezi Xue (HD) VERY CUTE Short Animation from MadArtistPublishing.com (MadArtistPublishing, Aug. 19, 2011)

https://www.youtube.com/watch?v=psZmAsH6I3Q

This two-minute video is a great example of how being flexible and allowing plans to evolve can lead to amazing experiences. We follow the relationship of a young boy and an older man (perhaps his grandfather) as they experience joy, worry, frustration, and happiness. A problem is solved creatively. The pace is slow and the emotions well portrayed. This video can also lead to a discussion exploring the frustrations that arise when we try to learn something new.

(4) Scrat-Gone Nutty (Blue Sky Studios, June 1, 2012)

https://www.youtube.com/watch?v=etKCHLgW_o0

This four-minute video portrays Scrat, the Ice Age sabertooth squirrel, trying to protect his precious stash of acorns. It reminds us how quickly circumstances and feelings can change. We don't always get the outcome we expect, but there are ways to adapt our changing environments to improve our situation. This is a good example of how even one character can experience many feelings quickly.

(5) Mariza—the Stubborn Donkey by Constantine Krystallis (OFFICIAL) (Constantine Krystallis, Oct. 13, 2009)

https://www.youtube.com/watch?v=_LmAcfO9lyg

In this four-and-a-half-minute video, we watch the unfolding story of a Greek fisherman and his donkey traveling up a hill to deliver a basket of fish. Their journey gives a snapshot of their relationship, displaying a wide range of feelings and bumps in relationships to which we can all relate.

(6) Dog and the Butcher—Aniboom Animation by Jonathan Holt (AniBOOM, Dec. 9, 2009)

https://www.youtube.com/watch?v=WplkcAlf7Y4

This video, slightly over two minutes in length, presents a great example of what can happen when two characters have very different ideas about something as well as what feelings can arise from a misunderstanding. Providing great practice in taking multiple perspectives and looking at relationships, the action in this YouTube video will have everyone enjoying the fun.

(7) Jumpstart—A Race to the Finish, Aniboom Animation by Simon Christen (July 19, 2008)

https://www.youtube.com/watch?v=2RiAN3IKGSM

As this two-minute video starts, we meet two characters, one of whom is pretty certain about the outcome of the approaching race. However, we find that things don't always work out as planned. This is a good video for talking about the feeling "okay" and handling disappointment.

(8) Twisted Dilsukhnagar Arena Award Winning 3D Animation Short Film (Funny Moments, Nov. 5, 2013)

https://www.youtube.com/watch?v=cyygnG6x-Wk

In this five-minute video, we watch as a pet owner struggles to come to grips with an unusual feature of his dog. He creatively tries to fix the problem and perseveres, but in the end he must face the truth that sometimes we have to accept what we may not like. This video has a nice, gentle pace with cute animation that everyone will enjoy.

(9) Pixar—Lifted (Pixar, May 23, 2010)

https://www.youtube.com/watch?v=pY1_HrhwaXU

This hilarious five-minute video looks at the frustrations of learning something new. A young alien on board a spaceship attempts to impress his teacher by beaming up a sleeping human, but his efforts are met with continual frustrations. This is a good example of a teacher/student relationship, portraying the feelings of both participants. The narrative is easy to follow and understand, and the music only adds to the humor of this short video.

(10) Sesame Street: Bert and Ernie in a Pyramid (Sesame Street, May 1, 2009)

https://www.youtube.com/watch?v=8yiqGtZXCmQ

In this five-minute Sesame Street video, Bert and Ernie explore a pyramid together. Ernie is overcome by fear inside the pyramid, but Bert is so eager to explore that he dismisses Ernie's anxiety and sets off on his own. This great clip reveals how people can be in the same situation but have very different feelings. Use this video to spark discussions about worries and uncomfortable situations.

(11) CGI Animated Short HD: "Space Invader" by Ian Cooke-Grimes (The CGBros, April 6, 2014)

https://www.youtube.com/watch?v=CMUzrOYMLYk

This two-and-a-half-minute video chronicles the invasion of a desert-like planet that has interesting residents by an egomaniacal alien who will stop at nothing for another conquest. However, beware of the power of a community in protecting its turf!

(12) Global Freezing Ice Age Imminent (Kim Hazel, May 8, 2009)

https://www.youtube.com/watch?v=4XRetwByfDY

In this two-minute video, we watch a dinosaur valiantly trying to prepare for the Ice Age. We can track the intensity of his feelings and thoughts as he tries to solve a problem that he thinks will keep him from the inevitable ending. It's short and fun.

(13) The Game of SPLEEF—Minecraft Animation—Slamacow (Slamacowcreations, Dec. 6, 2013)

https://www.youtube.com/watch?v=UqRSa30a7Ps

With no dialogue, this five-and-a-half-minute video allows viewers to pay attention to the nonverbal aspects of a narrative, such as reading facial expressions and relying on nonvisual information. Here are a couple of ancillary questions: What does the music tell you? Why is his stomach rumbling? Yes, we can find value in Minecraft.

(14) Finders Keepers (Robb Gibbs: The Ringling College of Art & Design, May 30, 2009)

https://www.youtube.com/watch?v=EH4kfO95hIA

In this amusing two-and-a-half-minute video, viewers follow two aliens as they attempt to dominate the planet on which they've landed. A race ensues, eventually leading to the destruction of the entire planet. This video serves as a great platform for discussion of the potential benefits, conflict, and feelings associated with competition and perseverance. This is a humorous video to jump-start the discussion of these important concepts.

(15) CGI Animated Short HD: "Playmate"—by Sen Liu & KunZhan Tao (The CGBros, July 9, 2014)

https://www.youtube.com/watch?v=2fR9HqilmKM

In slightly over three minutes, this video follows the relationship between a boy and his toy robot through the years. This is a good video for tracking how feelings between characters change over time and discussing how our actions can lead to changes in the feelings of those around us.

(16) Kre-O Battleship Alien Ambush (KREO Official, May 21, 2012)

https://www.youtube.com/watch?v=SKIC7_MmitI

The action-packed plot and use of language and dialogue make this four-and-a-half-minute video appealing and easy for older elementary school students to relate to. It's fast-paced, but the emotions are easy to identify and the plot develops quickly. This video has great examples of not giving up, even when frustrated. Witness the importance of teamwork as these soldiers work toward a unified goal—battling and defeating aliens.

(17) Egghunt (Paul Yan, Oct. 10, 2006)

https://www.youtube.com/watch?v=52M5EfRkBBo

This three-and-a-half-minute video humorously suggests that even cavemen struggled with relationships. Using only nonverbal information, this video lays a foundation for rich discussions of many aspects of social interaction. There's room for many different interpretations of what happens, so the discussion itself will often prove to be animated. Use it to explore feelings. There's a lot of richness here.

(18) "Wild Dogs"—Animated Short by Catherine Hicks (Catherine Hicks, May 2, 2009)

https://www.youtube.com/watch?v=sn2qepWagbc

In this two-and-a-half-minute video, two dogs (although I think the second one looks more like a cow) negotiate over bones in the desert. Two very different personalities are presented that can be identified and discussed, along with their motives and feelings. This provides a great way to initiate a discussion of tricking and someone getting what they deserve.

(19) 3D animation short "Bugs' Race" (Anna Jurkiewicz & Andrzej Ellert, Sept. 20, 2008)

https://www.youtube.com/watch?v=zw9AZ39s5LA

In this four-and-a-half-minute video, we watch a number of different characters as they progress (or not) along a racecourse. Everyone wants to win, but some try some questionable tricks to get ahead. You can track feelings but also discuss what is and isn't fair in racing. Everyone will have an opinion!

(20) "The Value of Breakfast"—Aniboom Animation (Hiren Solanki & Lian Pan, Nov. 12, 2012)

https://www.youtube.com/watch?v=1ZcYVVlXBC4

In this two-and-a-half-minute video, we watch two characters (who could easily be seen as siblings—it is interesting to see if students think the same) negotiating limited cereal and milk. The video includes many changes in feelings, hidden and obvious motives, and a surprising ending to keep students engaged and eager to enter discussion.

(21) Carrot Crazy (Logan Scelina, Aug. 15, 2011)

https://www.youtube.com/watch?v=7V7MOk0FZrg

In this amusing three-and-a-half-minute video, two hunters compete with each other to catch a rabbit. The situation escalates quickly as the hunters go to greater and greater lengths to impress and outdo each other. In the process, their initial goal of catching the rabbit is completely forgotten. In the end, *both* lose out on the bunny! This video portrays "jerky" and uncooperative behavior. The characters just don't know when to stop as the feelings of each hunter escalate in response to the other hunter's behavior.

(22) Michael Rutter—On the Level
(Michael Rutter, April 30, 2009)

https://www.youtube.com/watch?v=FtI9AiYWfeE

In this two-and-a-half-minute video, Bean Maxwell goes above and beyond to make the picture on his wall sit straight. However, his obsession with making it *perfectly* straight results in things getting completely out of hand. His feelings escalate along with his commitment to a losing cause. This is a great video to use when exploring the feelings associated with rigidity and an inability to accept imperfection.

(23) Les Pyramides d'Egypte—Animated Short Film
(Kheops Pyramides April 3, 2014)

https://www.youtube.com/watch?v=j6PbonHsqW0

Escape to an Egyptian archeological dig in the 1920s in this three-and-a-half-minute video. The archaeologist and his camel come across an interesting find. There's a lot of nonverbal communication, instances of "okay" feelings, and opportunities to relate feelings to thoughts and plans. This video is slower paced but very entertaining.

(24) Le Royaume (Nuno Alves-Rodrigues, Aug. 30, 2010)

https://www.youtube.com/watch?v=y6ZmMjMdrqs

In this four-minute video, a king pursues the biggest and best castle imaginable. His dissatisfaction (as well as unforeseen events) reflects his inability to be happy with what he has. Great facial expressions on the king and his workers give us an opportunity to discuss feelings associated with not getting what we want as well as dealing with anger in others. Lots of strong feelings, so preview carefully.

(25) Legacy—Animated Short Film
Savannah College of Art and Design (July 23, 2013)

https://www.youtube.com/watch?v=tl00xSaYOiI

In this four-minute coming of age story, we watch as a young man struggles with family expectations and intergenerational responsibilities. It's a bit sad but sure to bring up interesting discussions. It has a wonderful portrayal of feelings and a lot of nonverbal information. Again, preview carefully.

Are you ready to keep going? Read about YouCue activities in Chapter 4, and check out the list of which videos you can pair with specific activities in Appendix A. Also, start watching videos you've read about in this chapter, and think about how and with whom you can use them.

Chapter 4

YouCue Activities

This chapter contains 50 activities to accompany the online videos from the previous chapter, including:
- The Big Idea: A reminder that this book focuses on feelings
- Help It Happen: Introducing YCF to your students
- 25 Level 1 YouCues
- 25 Level 2 YouCues

The Big Idea

YouCues Levels 1 and 2 focus on expanding emotional vocabulary, tracking changes in feelings, and improving emotional self-reflection.

One goal of these activities is to expand the feeling words students know and use to label emotions. These include comfortable feelings (e.g., "happy," "interested," and "excited") as well as uncomfortable feelings (e.g., "angry," "sad," and "discouraged"). Studies tell us that uncomfortable feelings are more difficult to address, so you'll want to focus more on those.

We also want students to practice tracking how feelings change as what's happening changes. We rarely stay with one feeling state for long, so it's important to understand the fluidity of feelings. Finally, we want students to raise their comfort level with talking about their own feelings.

Help It Happen

When you introduce YCF to your students, discuss that we all experience lots of different feelings. Some of these feelings are comfortable, while others are uncomfortable. Ask students to name feelings—draw some pictures of feelings or make a list. Before watching, tell students that they'll be watching YouTube videos of characters having many different feelings. Tell them that after watching, you'll be doing some activities and talking about the feelings they notice.

When you get to the YouCue activities that work on tracking feelings, stop for some additional discussion. Spend some time talking about the idea of tracking, and explain that you'll be following how feelings of the characters change throughout the storyline. You might also give some examples of how your own feelings have changed that day. Perhaps you left the house feeling happy and excited about your day, but when you got up to your car, you noticed you had a flat. Uh oh, feeling change!

For both Level 1 and Level 2 YouCues, it's easiest to go through the activities sequentially. Because Level 2 activities often build on similar Level 1 activities, saving photos or other student work will make it easy to refresh their memories about what they accomplished earlier.

Remember that the two spreadsheets in Appendix A will help you match up the online videos with YouCues that work best together.

Here are some additional pointers about using the program with students:

- Pause and/or re-watch YouTube videos to support greater understanding through discussion.
- Don't use just one video or book—mixing it up keeps the work interesting and strengthens understanding.
- Think of these YouCues as a food court—there are many choices and *you* choose what looks best.
- Refer to Appendices A–D for helpful materials.
- For K–4th grade students you'll complete Level 1 YouCues with videos *and* with books. Please make the appropriate substitutions in YouCue vocabulary (e.g., substitute "book" for "video," "reading" for "watching," etc.) as necessary. Both terms aren't always provided in the activities listed.

YouCue Activities Level 1

Naming Feelings

Choose a YouTube video (or a book) you've previewed and think is the best starting place for your students. After watching (reading), work with students to generate a list of all the different comfortable and uncomfortable feelings they noticed. If the video or book has more than one character, you can make separate lists if you want.

Comfortable vs. Uncomfortable Feelings

Using the list of feelings made in the above YouCue "Namings Feelings", discuss how some feelings are comfortable and some are uncomfortable. During this activity, emphasize that we all have uncomfortable feelings sometimes. Discuss that our feelings can change quickly, so in a short amount of time we can experience many different emotions (e.g., "mad" quickly followed by "sad," or "excited" quickly followed by "disappointed").

Sort your collection of emotional words into comfortable and uncomfortable lists (Illustration 7). Emphasize how many different feelings there are on their lists. Remember to re-watch or re-read if you think that would aid comprehension or generate more feeling vocabulary. If students begin to talk about their own experiences with some of these feelings, allow the discussion to go in that direction. Encourage others to share their thoughts and/or talk about when they had some of these feelings as well. If it seems like a good time to ask them to draw some of these experiences, do it. That's going ahead to Level 2 activities, but it's okay. Repeat this activity after watching other videos. You can start a summary list of feelings vocabulary for future use, divided into comfortable and uncomfortable feelings.

comfortable	uncomfortable
proud	frustrated
victorious	scared
confident	disappointed
grateful	discouraged
	threatened

Illustration 7.
Older elementary school students listing feelings after viewing a YouTube video.

Sketch a Feeling

After watching a video (or reading a book), encourage students to draw one picture of a character experiencing a comfortable *or* an uncomfortable feeling. Encourage them to include relevant contextual details: who (including multiple characters when appropriate), where (this can be hard, so work slowly to encourage details), when, as well as the action. If students start to elaborate on feelings of multiple characters, that's great—use it as the basis for discussion about how characters influence each other, not just their feelings but thoughts and actions as well. If they want to draw more, you can use the YouCue *Contrasting Feelings* for your next activity.

"Okay" Is a Feeling

Introduce and discuss the feeling "okay." This is often overlooked as we teach students about emotions but is critical in social interaction, learning, and self-regulation. Watch a YouTube video looking for moments when a character is feeling "okay." Younger students may enjoy holding up an "okay" sticker or expression taped to a Popsicle stick when they think the character is feeling "okay." If there are multiple characters, students can track each one separately or split into groups to monitor multiple characters. Students can also look for times when both characters feel "okay." Although this YouCue isn't directly about tracking feelings, mention that this activity focuses on watching how feelings change and noticing these changes. They'll be doing more of this when they get to the *Tracking 1 & 2* YouCues.

Feelings & Thoughts

After watching a YouTube video uninterrupted, view it again, stopping for students to identify thoughts of characters. You can write or draw thoughts on sticky notes and put them above the character's head when you freeze a video frame. If you're watching a video with more than one character, develop thought bubbles for each— this is work on perspective taking. You can add feelings as well, reminding students that characters don't always share the same feeling. Again, these visuals support social understanding.

Inner Voice Level 1

Introduce the idea that sometimes we talk to ourselves in our heads. Give some examples from your life. Include both supportive comments (e.g., "I can do it!") as well as somewhat critical ones (e.g., "I can't believe I did that!"). Watch a YouTube video all the way through. Then re-watch, pausing at times when you think the character might be hearing his or her "inner voice." Write down possible comments, supporting students in thinking about contextual information and feeling state (Illustration 8). Discuss the tone of the inner voices. Were some positive or helpful? Were some critical and upsetting? What feeling state did they reflect? Use several different videos because this is an important concept.

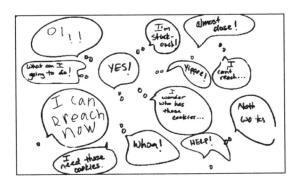

Illustration 8. Student work for inner thought bubbles.

Feelings Come in Sizes

Using previous work, discuss how feelings come in sizes. Sort the feeling words you've talked about by size. For younger students, you can talk about "a little bit sad" and "really big sad." With older students, use more specific emotional vocabulary (e.g., "a little bit angry" = "annoyed"). Have feelings lists (Appendix C) available so students can explore new vocabulary. Develop 1–5 scales, in which 1 represents a small expression of a feeling (e.g., "annoyed") and 5 represents a large expression of feeling (e.g., "furious").

Take this activity slowly—you want students to be developing a solid emotional vocabulary, so allow for a lot of discussion and use visual supports. Watch some additional videos, encouraging students to discuss feeling sizes and the emotional vocabulary you've developed.

Bunches of Feelings

We often experience combinations of feelings. For example, when we see someone coming with a present for us we might feel "happy" ("yeah!"), "excited" ("wonder what it is?"), and "nervous" ("hope I like it") pretty much at the same time. Such layers of feelings add richness to experiences but can be difficult to recognize. Watch a YouTube video and discuss and/or have students draw about times when characters might have been feeling combinations of feelings, both comfortable and uncomfortable. Feel free to pause on frames that show emotions, and let students look at those while they think and discuss.

Contrasting Feelings

Ask students to choose one comfortable feeling *and* one uncomfortable feeling that a character experienced. Have them draw two sketches contrasting the situations (Illustration 9). Encourage sharing and discussion. Again, if students begin to talk about their own experiences and feelings, allow the discussion to move to that more personal level.

Illustration 9. Younger elementary students writing examples of thought bubbles associated with feelings.

Interjection Injector #1

Using notes you made in *Feelings & Thoughts*, re-watch the video. Suggest that sometimes our thoughts aren't full sentences. They can be short phrases or interjections (Appendix D). Give some examples of when you might have an interjection as a thought reaction to some event (e.g., I slip and fall. My first thought might be "aaaahhhhh!!" rather than "I tripped on that step"). Interjections are also important because when we listen to others, popping in with appropriate interjections lets others know we're listening and we understand their emotional state (this is a form of empathy).

Students with social learning challenges often don't use such interjections or short phrases. This is a way to practice. Watch a YouTube video and pause, allowing students to fill in the moment with a short phrase or interjection from the list. Point out that interjections pair with feelings and reflect feeling size. You can add sticky notes with the interjection as a thought bubble and a feeling label. For this YouCue, make sure you use visual supports. Students may make an incorrect interjection choice (e.g., choosing "yeah!" when a better choice would be "yikes"). Such errors are usually based on a misinterpretation or lack of attention to feeling state.

Interjection Injector #2

Reviewing your list of interjections, remind students that interjections can encapsulate a feeling. As a video plays, encourage students to call out appropriate interjections from the list as a running commentary. Turn off the dialogue or music if it's distracting. This can be a fun activity; just make sure everyone stays regulated so things don't get out of control!

Interjection Injector #3

Once students understand the idea behind interjections, encourage them to use them watching YouTube videos *without the lists of interjections*. Students can make sketches of scenes they remember in which a character struggled (this works really well with books) and insert a stick figure that provides the interjection. You can bring in the concept of empathy, asking students to have the stick figure "say something that would help the character feel better" (Illustration 10).

Illustration 10. Student drawing of a character feeling with the insertion of himself as a stick figure encouraging the character.

Who Cares? Level 1 (for YouTube videos that have more than one character)

Sometimes in our desire to get what we want we neglect others. Review this idea, watch a YouTube video, and then lead a discussion on how the character failed to pay attention to someone else's feelings and/or words. Focus discussion on the feelings of all the participants, and support the group in identifying what factors were at play (Illustration 11). Encourage students to identify the repercussions of not paying attention to the thoughts and feelings of others. Come up with options the character might have considered and how this would have changed things.

Illustration 11. Using Kimochis ™ feelings with characters sketch for Who Cares? Level one YouCue.

Stuck Level 1

When we get stuck on an idea, we may have trouble moving forward, changing what we're doing, or accepting the status quo and knowing when to quit. Review this idea, watch a YouTube video, and then lead a discussion about how the character feels as a result of being stuck. What are the pros and cons of being committed to making something happen? How does determination relate to knowing when you've tried enough? Have students draw sets of pictures, one of how the character is stuck and one offering another choice.

Got Worries? Level 1

Like all feelings, worries come in sizes. As worries become larger, they may seem to take over and be impossible to contain. Root your discussion with an example or two from your life (not *too* big). Then watch a YouTube video and discuss the worries of the character.

What size were they? How did the character respond? Were there options? Students can make sketches of the character worries, comparing and discussing their drawings. If students bring up their own worries, incorporate them into your discussions, making sketches to support the group process (Illustration 12).

> Our worries
>
> Tom: worries about Mom being late
> Mark: worries about going to Jack's house
> Jeffrey: worries about taking a shower
> Jules: worries about loud music

Illustration 12. These students decided to make a list of what each of them worries about. They were ready to talk about themselves!

Outer Coach Level 1 (for YouTube videos with more than one character)

Sometimes everyone needs support to get through a rough moment. Give an example of when someone helped you with some advice or encouragement. Watch a video and discuss the help a character received from the outside. Was it hard for the character to accept help? Did the encouragement help him or her succeed? What feelings (or combinations of feelings) were involved? As always, suggest that students draw about what they noticed from the video to use as a basis for discussion.

Hard Day Sketch Level 1

We all have days when it seems the hard times just keep coming. Introduce the notion of "the straw that broke the camel's back" in a way that your students can understand. Include how difficult it can be to see any good in a day that challenges us. Watch a video, and discuss a character's feelings, attempts to recover, and empathic comments that might have been helpful. (Interjections work well here.) Make sketches as needed.

Take a Chance Level 1

Worries, apprehensions, or a lack of experience can make us unwilling to take risks. We may be afraid of making a mistake. This is an important concept for students with social learning difficulties, so take some time with this YouCue, and perhaps repeat it with several videos and books. Watch a YouTube video, and ask students to sketch times when a character was worried and did or didn't take a risk. Encourage thought and feeling bubbles. Sequences of two or three sketches are great for this YouCue. Remind students that sometimes taking a chance gets us only partially to our goal and can lead to disappointment. Taking a chance connects with inner voice and determination, so weave those ideas into your discussions and sketches. Focus on all those feelings.

Oooops! Level 1

We all make mistakes. Mistakes can be proof that we're brave and trying new things. They can also reflect poor choices, lack of understanding of context or other people's perspective, and impulsivity, among other factors. Watch a YouTube video, then ask students to sketch one mistake a character made, and discuss. Probe to get information about the size of the mistake, the feelings involved, and how the character responded to his or her mistake.

Tracking #1

Tracking YouCues are about developing visual supports to portray how much and how quickly feelings change. Keep this in mind as you develop your visuals. After watching a YouTube video, ask students to draw a picture (or do one together) of a character experiencing a *comfortable* feeling (remember to include contextual details), and then a picture of what happened before and what happened next. Did that change how the character felt? Did it make the character feel better? Okay? Worse? Look at other moments in the video. Sketch and discuss.

Tracking #2

Ask students to draw a picture (or do one together) of a character experiencing an *uncomfortable* feeling, and then a picture of what happened before and what happened next. Did that change how the character felt? Did it make the character feel better? Okay? Worse?

Include contextual information. Look at other moments in the video. Sketch and discuss.

This can get complicated when there's more than one character. If that's the case, you may want to draw larger pictures that include both characters, labeling how they're each feeling. Use emotional vocabulary that's as precise as possible (Illustration 13). This is also a great place to add thought and speaking bubbles for differing perspectives. Your visual supports will be full of important social information because you're building sequences that show how feeling states change based on what's happening.

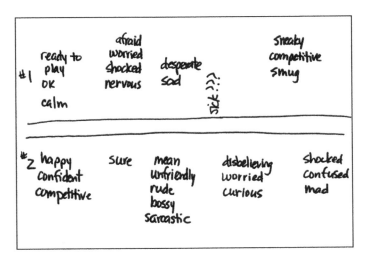

Illustration 13. Rather than sketching, these middle school students made lists tracking the feelings of two characters.

Piles of Feelings

For this activity you'll need some colored tokens or Popsicle sticks. Assign colors to families of feelings—perhaps red for "angry" feelings, yellow for "sad" feelings, blue for "okay" feelings, and green for "happy" feelings. Label containers or make piles for these feelings. As students watch a video, have them put tokens in the appropriate piles. Afterwards, talk about which feelings were more prevalent and why and how many times feelings changed between the categories.

Relationships Level 1 (for YouTube videos with more than one character)

Examine some of your completed work from *Tracking #1 and Tracking 2*. Encourage discussion comparing the feeling shifts between characters. How did one character's feelings influence the other character's feelings? Emphasize how both characters' thoughts and feelings contributed to this great story, how there were so many feelings over a short period of time, and how the emotional shifts and actions of each character affected the other. In upcoming packs of YouCues (see the "Coming Up" section of Chapter 1), you'll revisit some of this work as you delve into relationship concepts such as "cooperation" and "repairing bumps," but feel free to bring in those ideas now.

Watch & Think Level 1

This YouCue involves putting together everything discussed in previous Level 1 YouCues. Watch videos (either re-watch or see new ones), and ask students for their thoughts. What worked; what didn't work? What did they notice about feelings and feeling shifts? What did they find interesting? Did they like or dislike a particular character? You'll find yourself talking about much more than feelings, and that's great!

Graph It

Because quite a few students with social learning challenges do well in math, the idea behind *Graph It* is to apply a visual, mathematical concept to tracking emotions. You'll use the comfortable and uncomfortable feeling scales that you developed in the *Feelings Come in Sizes* activity as the *y-coordinate* and time as the *x-coordinate*. Prepare the template—the vertical axis has comfortable feelings on the positive portion, uncomfortable feelings on the negative. Again, the horizontal axis is time. Choose one character at a time and watch the YouTube video again, stopping at places where emotions shifted. Demonstrate how to add dots to the graph at each point to show the feeling changes. Support students in noticing small shifts in intensity that may build up to a strong feeling. Then re-watch for the second character.

You can use a separate template or use different colored markers on one template to differentiate characters, depending on your students (graphing both on one template is visually "busier," but has the benefit of being able to see if the two characters are in sync emotionally). You can also put the templates in sheet protectors and draw on the sheet protector—that will allow you to overlay the two graphs for easier comparison.

This might sound somewhat complicated, but take a look at the student examples in Illustrations 14 and 15. It's really pretty easy. Discuss what these graphs tell about the feeling shifts. Emphasize how quickly characters moved between comfortable and uncomfortable feelings.

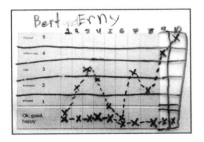

Illustration 14. An example of tracking two characters in an overlay.

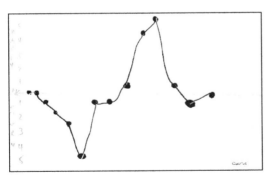

Illustration 15. An example of tracking a single character's feelings.

At this point, keep using the above YouCue activities until you've completed:
At least 5 YouCues with YouTube videos
AND
5 YouCues with books (K–4th grade)
OR
At least 8 YouCues with YouTube videos (5th–8th grade)

Then, you're ready to move on to YouCues Level 2

YouCue Activities Level 2

Feelings of Others We Know

Ask students to remember a time when someone they know (perhaps a sibling, classmate, or even a parent) experienced an uncomfortable feeling. Have them draw a picture about that experience. If they can't think of one, encourage them to make one up. This is more about working with uncomfortable feelings than having accurate recollections. Share and discuss as a group. If students talk about what happened next for that person, let them. Ask students how these uncomfortable feelings were handled and what self-talk might have been involved. These discussions can develop a life of their own!

Self-Sketching #1

Share your own example of a time when you felt happy, excited, or okay. Sketch what happened in a series of pictures, labeling your feelings and thoughts (remember those interjections) throughout. Then, ask students to think of a time when they experienced a comfortable feeling. Have them draw a sequence of what happened. Did feelings ever change? Was there ever an uncomfortable feeling? Continue as long as students want. If another person was in their example, encourage them to include that person's feelings. That will enrich this activity.

Self-Sketching #2

Share your own example of a time when you felt upset, mad, or sad. Draw what happened in a series of pictures, labeling your feelings throughout, and discuss any feeling changes that occurred. Bring out one of the lists of uncomfortable feelings your students made during Level 1 activities. Ask them to select one of those feeling words and draw a sketch of when they experienced that feeling. Encourage older students to choose examples that go beyond the basic feelings of "mad" and "sad" (e.g., "scared," "nervous," "furious"). Did feelings change at any point? Did they grow larger or smaller? If another person was in their example, include that person. That will allow you to focus more on what was happening in the relationship.

If students can't think of a personal example, see if they can come up with an example of someone they know (e.g., a sibling, a classmate) being upset. Lead a discussion on how our feelings change a lot, just like the characters in the videos. When students describe their uncomfortable feelings (Illustration 16), ask other group members if they might have felt the same way. How did things work out? Encourage discussion!

Illustration 16. A self-sketch of an uncomfortable feeling during the day.

Self-Reflection #1

The emphasis of this YouCue is on tools to handle uncomfortable feelings. As a group, lead a discussion about what strategies we can use to handle uncomfortable emotions. Remind students about the feeling "okay" that they studied in Level 1. Encourage discussion about how they can get to okay-ness from an uncomfortable feeling. For further information, you may want to refer to *The Zones of Regulation* (Kuypers, 2011) for great information about tools to maintain regulation and handle feelings.

Who Cares? Level 2

Remind students of the work in *Who Cares? Level 1*. Watch a YouTube video for review. Ask students to sketch an example of when they themselves or someone they know didn't pay attention to the feelings or words of another. Ask them to include everyone who was involved and expand their single sketch into a series, with thought and talk bubbles as well as feeling labels. Focus discussion on the feelings of all the participants, and support the group in discussing what factors were at play. Encourage students to identify the repercussions of not paying attention to the thoughts and feelings of others and come up with options they might have considered.

Stuck Level 2

Review your *Stuck Level 1* work. Ask students to sketch an example of when they themselves or someone they know became stuck on an idea. Ask them to include everyone who was involved and expand their single sketch into a series, with thought and talk bubbles as well as feeling labels (Illustration 17). Focus discussion on the feelings of all the participants as well as how rigidity or black-and-white thinking was a factor. Ask them about how they felt when they were stuck. Did they realize they were being rigid? Did they try to become flexible? Were they successful or not? Did others try to help? Can they come up with options they might have tried? Refer back to your discussions in *Self-Reflection #1*.

Probe deeper with questions. What are the pros and cons of being committed to making something happen? How does determination relate to knowing when you've tried enough? How often do they think they get stuck?

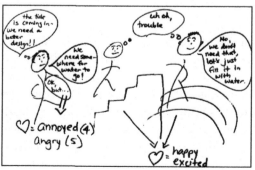

Illustration 17. Student series of four illustrations of a time when he was stuck on his own idea. Numbers represent intensity of emotion.

Got Worries? Level 2

Review your discussion from *Got Worries? Level 1* and watch a YouTube video. Ask students to sketch some of their worries (or those of someone they know if they're unable to draw their own). Students can judge the size of these worries, think about tools they can use when these worries arise, and provide support, empathy, and suggestions to each other. This activity also provides the opportunity to talk about being a kind, good friend, even if someone has worries that you might think are silly or stupid.

Outer Coach Level 2

Review a YouTube video or give your own example of outer coach. Ask students to draw an example of when they benefited from an outer coach. If students struggle, ask them if they've ever been in a situation when a parent or other adult helped them. Encourage sharing, as well as discussion of feelings, type of help received, its benefits, and what they might do if a similar situation arose again. You can focus on feelings before and after the outer coaching was given.

Empathy #1

Continue your work with interjections by asking students to be empathic to group members as they share their sketches and experiences. Have the interjections list available, but also include short phrases such as "too bad," "oh, no," etc. Brainstorm what might be an empathic statement in various situations. If your students are sketching, you can pass around the sketches and have students draw themselves into the picture as a stick figure and add an empathic comment.

Feelings of the Day

Encourage students to talk about comfortable *and* uncomfortable feelings they felt that day. You can go first with an example. Discuss definitions of emotional vocabulary as needed. Did they feel more than one at the same time? If you usually start sessions with some "what's new?" conversation, just add the feelings component. If needed, remind students that we all feel uncomfortable feelings every day (Illustration 18). If students can't think of an uncomfortable feeling or state that they were happy all day, don't push them. As they listen to peers talk about uncomfortable feelings, they'll begin to feel more ready to do the same (although perhaps not on Day 1).

Illustration 18. Student description of comfortable and uncomfortable feelings they experienced when bowling. Everyone could relate!

Empathy #2

Encourage continued practice of empathic interjections in less structured activities and contexts. Emphasize that an interjection is a short pop-in, not a long sentence or narration. It's not about talking about yourself, and using interjections lets the speaker know you're listening and you care.

Students may have a hard time judging whether someone else's experience calls for comfortable or uncomfortable interjections—that's due to struggles with perspective taking and identifying feeling states of others. When you hear spontaneous empathy, remember to compliment students on their growing skills.

Hard Day Self-Sketching

Again, lead by example. Talk about a day you had that seemed filled with tough moments and uncomfortable feelings, such as rain, traffic, a broken printer, spilled coffee on the phone, etc. Discuss how experiences and feelings piled up, how hard it was to keep moving forward, how discouraged you began feeling, and so on. Include how you hung in there, including any self-talk examples. You can describe it as an "Ormie" day (see that video). Draw visual supports of the sequence of your day including thoughts and feelings (Illustration 19). Then encourage students to come up with their own examples. Make sure they include feelings! Discuss…

Illustration 19. Student series sketch of a difficult time with a sibling and parent.

Hard Day Feelings Sizes

Using the sketches from *Hard Day Self-Sketching*, work with students as they label the sizes of their feelings (e.g., you can use a 1–5 scale as in Dunn Buron & Curtis, 2012). Also encourage them to choose feeling vocabulary that reflects the size of the emotions from your work in Level 1.

Hard Day Recovery

Work with sketches from *Hard Day Self-Sketching* and *Hard Day Feelings Sizes* to support students in examining how they handled the difficult points of their day. Were there any positive or pleasant events or interactions? Were they able to resolve difficulties, either by being flexible, admitting to a mistake, or by taking a chance? Encourage students to reflect on how they feel *right now*. Have they recovered from their bad day, or do they still need to do some work coming to grips with what happened? If so, how did they recover? If not, what might be helpful?

Take a Chance Level 2

Revisit the notion of taking chances, being brave, trusting in yourself and others, and using tools to support such learning. Give some examples of when you took a risk and it worked out, it didn't work out, and it partially worked out. Ask students to make some sketches of risks they or someone they know took.

Remind students that a small risk is still a risk to be appreciated, especially when taking chances doesn't come easily. Focus on feelings before, during, and after. Were others involved? What did the student think initially about the challenge? Did that thought prove to be accurate or not?

Ask students to rate the difficulty level of chance-taking opportunities before undertaking it and afterwards. This can help students understand that we often exaggerate the complexity of a task as well as our perceived ineptitude.

Provide opportunities to take chances during your general work. Some possibilities are new or hard games, building challenges (e.g., making a building for another student to knock down with Koosh balls), charades (many students with social learning challenges shy away from these), or putting on a performance. Rate difficulty levels before and after and discuss your students' level of success.

Oooops Level 2

Students with social learning challenges struggle with mistakes. Often black-and-white thinkers, they code actions in life as right or wrong. Correct or incorrect. Good or bad. They may see mistakes of others as intentional rather than accidental. It takes lots of conversation to understand the role mistakes play in our lives.

For now, focus on the feelings that accompany mistakes, either the ones we make ourselves or the ones we witness. Ask students to sketch mistakes they've made or seen. Probe for clear feeling vocabulary. Mistakes can often be stretched out in time as we struggle or interact with others. During that time, our feelings (and those of others) often escalate. If students express the notion that making mistakes is hard, agree. It is!

Self-Tracking

Watch a video about tracking feelings as a warm-up. Use series of sketches students made in previous Level 2 activities, or make new ones. Support students in looking at the big picture of feeling states. How did their feelings shift over time? How much flux was there between comfortable and uncomfortable feelings? What was the range of particular feelings? Were there times when they felt okay? Do these patterns tell them anything about themselves (e.g., they get very angry or frustrated quickly, they get angry first, explode, and then feel sad). Self-reflection about feeling states is a process (Illustration 20). Even short discussions lead to learning.

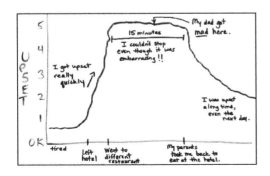

Illustration 20. **Student graph depicting how he got upset during a family trip. Now he's more ready to think and talk about his reactions.**

Inner Voice Level 2

Watch a YouTube video, and review previous work around inner voice. Using sketches from previous Level 2 activities, brainstorm with students about what their inner voice may have been saying (Illustrations 21 & 22). Remind students that inner voices sometimes use interjections, so get that list out if it will be helpful. Discuss the tone of the inner voices. Were some positive and encouraging? Were some critical and upsetting? Which were most helpful? Did any make things worse?

Illustration 21.
A student's work describing his feelings and inner thoughts while playing a board game.

Illustration 22.
A student's depiction of his inner voice. This sketch gives crucial information about his inner conflicts, depression, and anxiety.

Describe, Describe, Describe!

In your daily work with students, emphasize descriptive emotional vocabulary. Incorporate this activity into educational settings (language arts, PE), home (dinner conversation, watching TV), car rides (commenting on others you see), and recreational locations (at the airport, in line at Legoland) as appropriate. Use rich emotional vocabulary yourself. Ask students if they can relate to feelings (and sizes of feelings) you mention (Illustration 23). Ask them about feelings of others (characters in books, friends from the park). Wonder how they may have felt when they tell you about a problem or conflict. (Note: Saying "I wonder..." is a great way to ask a question. It implies that you want to know but aren't sure of the answer.) Compliment precise use of emotional labels.

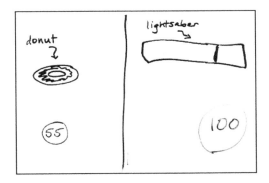

Illustration 23. This preschooler showed how he is moderately happy (55)) when he got a donut and super happy (100) when he got a lightsaber. Good work on judging the size of his feelings!

Relationships Level 2

Examine completed work from *Self-Tracking*. Encourage reflection and discussion about how feelings shifted between the student and whoever else was present. How did one person's actions and feelings influence the other person? Emphasize emotional shifts and their impacts on participants. How did things end up? Was everyone satisfied, or was there no clear resolution? If the event involved an adult, was the adult trying to be helpful? Or was there a conflict reflecting differing perspectives? This can lead to a discussion about how issues between people aren't always quickly resolved and that relationships are always changing.

Watch & Think Level 2 (best for groups and classrooms)

This YouCue involves putting everything discussed in Level 2 YouCues together. Prep students before an activity that afterwards you'll be talking about how the feelings that accompanied successes and challenges arose. Videotaping is helpful because it can be difficult for students to remember exactly what happened. Watch these videos, and ask students for their thoughts. Remember to include moments when students were showing their skills. Once again, focus on feeling states and what helped to maintain good feelings as well as what happened when uncomfortable feelings were evident.

Ask younger students to make sketches of how they worked and/or played together, of course including feelings. If instances of mistakes, chance-taking, worrying, rigidity, or outer coaching show up, make sure to spend a bit of time with those. Make visual supports for all to see.

Game Time!

Before playing a competitive board game, make individual 1–5 happy/okay, mad, sad, and worried scales for each student (Illustration 23). As they play the game, ask them to mark changes in feeling states. When any uncomfortable feeling gets to a 3 or higher, stop and brainstorm tools to recover. Encourage support from other students. Afterwards, discuss how much feelings shifted throughout the game.

Illustration 23.
Multiple feeling scales before and when in use to monitor feelings during a game. As feelings escalate, stop for discussion!

Take a Breath

In everyday interactions involving conflict, slow things down and support students in labeling how *others* are feeling and what *others* are thinking and planning. Students may tell you their own feelings and thoughts and plans. Try to get them to stay in the moment, remind them that it's *their* feeling or thought, and support them in figuring out what their friend wants and feels. Again, this is based in perspective taking (and staying regulated), so it will take practice. Compliment and encourage them as they begin to figure out this important information.

Walk the Line

Give students a structured challenge activity tailored to their interests. My favorites are a building activity (e.g., making a destructible fortress using all kinds of blocks, creating a Rube Goldberg machine, or building a structure from a Cranium Megabuilder kit) or imaginary play (e.g., setting up a restaurant, zoo, or neighborhood). The structure of a goal keeps the pressure on; you want students needing to communicate and combine their ideas and materials. If you want to add another complication, ask students to work together in silence for a certain number of minutes. They'll need to depend on nonverbal communication; that will make the cooperating even harder.

Before starting, spend some time identifying what problems and feelings might arise and how they can be managed. Remember to make a visual support with this information as well as what the goal will look like when complete (provide executive function support as needed). Watch students to see if they refer to it themselves, or refer them to it if they need support. Discuss their observations and yours afterwards. If you film some of it, you can review the video. Be sure to point out what they did well as well as how challenges were overcome. Support discussions of difficult moments.

Graph It Level 2

In your day-to-day activities or when students talk about an event that includes important feelings, ask them to graph their own experience like they did for characters in *Graph It Level 1*. Share an example from your own life as an example, and graph it out. Remember to include both comfortable and uncomfortable feelings. Use the graphs to support students in critically describing the flux of feelings. Look to other group members for empathy and supportive comments.

Chapter 5

Moving Ahead

By now, you may be thinking about choosing some new YouTube videos or books to use with the YouCues in this book or about developing your own YouCue activities. This chapter contains some tips that I've picked up in my YCF journey. If you have questions along the way (or want to share your finds and activities), feel free to check www.socialtime.org to send an email. Sharing within our community is a wonderful way to recognize that we all have great ideas.

I find videos by trolling YouTube. This takes time, patience, and a sense of humor. Once you find a YouTube video you like, suggestions of other YouTube videos pop up in the sidebar. While some may work, you also can quickly find yourself far afield viewing completely inappropriate videos. If this happens, just retreat quickly.

I developed the YouCues through a lot of trial and error. Some of my ideas worked, and some absolutely didn't (students were quick to tell me). However, it's not rocket science. As you went through YCF, you probably already had a number of great ideas. *By thinking through what you want to achieve, you'll find it fun to experiment with your own ideas.*

Selecting Your Own YouTube Videos (or books)

As you watch videos (or look for new books to expand your library), here are some things to keep in mind:

Look for good relationships and storylines. Consider how visually "busy" the work looks. Too many images may distract from the focus on relationships.

Look for quality portrayal of emotions. Don't settle for something in which emotions look vague or unclear. Hold out for the great animators and artists!

Look for stories in which problems are faced and solved. This provides material to work on many different social cognitive concepts.

I use videos that are about three to six minutes in length. That allows you to have more time for discussion.

Consider pacing. Children who need more time to process do best with YouTube videos that move at a slower pace. Conversely, some students respond better to a lot of action. Always think of your audience.

I favor YouTube videos without dialogue—it just seems easier. Make sure the storyline is easily understood through contextual and nonverbal information. With books, you don't always have to read it as it's written, especially if text gets too complicated.

Be mindful of ratings, questionable language, and scary elements, even for older students.

After you've chosen a YouTube video or book and shared it with students, ask them if they liked it. They'll tell you, and it's good to listen to their feedback, even if you spent hours finding what you thought were great videos.

While there are many great animators, there are some animation studios that I particularly like. If you subscribe to them, they'll email you links as new videos are released. Of course, not all of them will work, but check out:

- aniBoom Animation
- The CGBros
- Brigham Young University Center for Animation
- Ringling College of Art and Design Animation

Designing Your Activities

When I first started developing YouCue Feelings, I wrote specific activities for specific videos. Soon however, I found that most, if not all, activities applied to multiple videos. I ended watching videos I really liked and coming up with activities that I could then use with other videos. New videos gave me ideas that I hadn't considered before. *It's also likely that, as you watch videos preselected in YCF, you'll come up with ideas that I didn't. Great!* As you experiment, here are some points you may want to consider.

- Why do I especially like this YouTube video?
- How else can I use this video to support emotional development?
- What features stand out from a social learning perspective?
- Is this a video where things go smoothly as characters demonstrate flexibility, joint problem solving, and recognition of each other's feelings? If so, it could support activities that focus on what we can do to help relationships run smoothly and discuss comfortable feelings.
- Or, is this a video with many bumps, conflicts, and challenges? Then, it could support activities that focus on the difficulties that can come up between people and how we can deal with these issues as well as the uncomfortable feelings that may arise.
- Of course, it could be a great video that shows both—relationships working and relationships stumbling. In some ways, those are the best because you can do so much with them.
- Always consider what visual supports you'll use or will have students create. Their active participation, even before discussion starts, is an important step in the learning process. Illustrations also let you gauge student understanding.
- Plan your tasks and formulate some ways to cue discussion, but be prepared to be flexible and use teachable moments as they occur.
- What you may think is a great activity may be too much, too complicated. You may need to break down your great idea into two or more activities. Don't try to cover too much. Remember, these ideas are complicated for students with social learning challenges.
- In your everyday work, think about what social learning concepts students don't fully understand. That's how I began to develop YouCues to teach about "cooperation" (coming out soon).

Of course, students make the best critics. They may have wonderful and supportive ideas or less positive opinions. Remember, we can maintain our own flexibility and manage our own feelings about what they say. We'll be setting a great example for them.

I've thoroughly enjoyed using YouTube videos with the wonderful children and families I'm fortunate to know. Whether you incorporate these videos into your work a lot or just a little, I hope you'll enjoy exploring this vast library of work that is YouTube. Happy viewing!

Appendix A

Appendices A-1 http://tinyurl.com/qhrwzwu (for Level 1 YouCues) and A-2 http://tinyurl.com/n4yzfeb (for Level 2 YouCues) are spreadsheets designed to help you match YouTube videos with YouCue Activities. These are large spreadsheets due to the number of videos and YouCues, so they are available online for easier use. Use the links above to see them on your computer.

Appendix B

Book Recommendations

You probably have lots of terrific books in your library already that you can use with the YouCue Feelings program. If you want additional titles, here are some of my favorites:

Duck in the Truck by Jez Alborough: A well-known, simple story that's good for reviewing basic emotions.

Fly Guy (series) by Tedd Arnold: Students love this series, perhaps because of its uncluttered look and focus on the relationship between two characters.

When Sophie Gets Angry—Really, Really Angry... by Molly Bang: This classic story can serve as a base for discussions about self-regulating tools.

A Bedtime for Bear by Bonny Becker: Bear and Mouse are trying to get ready for bed, each in their own way. Great for tracking the feelings of two characters in reaction to each other.

Itty Bitty by Cece Bell: Short and uncomplicated book that's great for some basic feelings identification.

Calvin Can't Fly by Jennifer Berne: Very well-written book about being different from others. Great to support discussions about liking things others around you don't. Nice ending about community pulling together.

In the Town All Year 'Round by Rotraut Susanne Berner: Beautiful book without text that follows a community over four seasons. Wonderful for work relating feelings to what's happening.

The Chocolate-Covered-Cookie Tantrum by Deborah Blumenthal: Probably my favorite book about a young child getting angry. Young kids love it!

Sometimes You Get What You Want by Lisa Brown and Meredith Gary: And other times you don't get what you want. Lots of nice examples to start discussions about feelings and preferences.

Cross-country Cat by Mary Calhoun: A Siamese cat braves a snowy forest in his efforts to get home. But the woods can be a dangerous place…

Fortunately by Remy Charlip: A classic book in which feelings change on every page.

The Blue Ribbon Day by Katie Couric: Two good friends learn that each of them is good at different things.

The Day the Crayons Quit by Drew Daywalt: Crayons in a box revolt, each for their own reason and feeling.

Hunter's Best Friend at School (series) by Laura Malone Elliott: Fabulous for feelings and feeling tracking! Hunter tries to deal with his best friend Stripe's poor choices.

Mean Soup by Betsy Everitt: A mom helps her son deal with his difficult day in an interesting way.

The Day Louis Got Eaten by John Fardell: Sarah has to save her little brother from a sequence of monsters. Funny and suspenseful.

Muncha! Muncha! Muncha! by Candace Fleming: Mr. McGreely tries to defend his garden against attacking bunnies. His feelings and solutions get bigger and bigger!

Tiger Can't Sleep by S.J. Fore: A favorite for many! An adorable tiger lives in a boy's closet but can't seem to settle down for the night. Great to track feelings of anger getting bigger and bigger.

Don't Forget to Come Back by Robie Harris: A young girl cajoles and threatens her parents in her attempt to keep them from going out. If you're looking for a book about a family with great art on their walls and parents who dress up to go to the opera, this book's for you!

Aki and the Fox by Akiko Hayashi: Gorgeous illustrations of feelings in this book my mother gave to my daughter about the adventures of a young Japanese girl and her plush friend Kon. Great range of feelings to track in this book that's one of my favorites!

Princess Hyacinth (The Surprising Tale of a Girl Who Floated) by Florence Parry Heide: Wonderful story about a Princess weighed down so she won't float. This story is wonderful to get students thinking about what worries weigh them down.

Owen by Kevin Henkes: Owen loves his blankie but his parents think it's time to take it away. Interesting ending that will lead to lots of discussion.

Wemberly Worried by Kevin Henkes: Wemberly has lots of worries! Students can try to figure out how she might be helped.

My Lucky Day by Keiko Kasza: Fox thinks he's got a pork roast in his future but Piglet doesn't make it easy. The underlying twist and tricky ending will challenge your social learners.

The Pig's Picnic by Keiko Kasza: Pig's friends try to spruce him up for a date with Miss Pig but she has an unexpected (?) reaction.

The Wolf's Chicken Stew by Keiko Kasza: An uncomplicated very cute story about a wolf who changes his mind about eating a family of chickens.

Where Is the Cake? by T.T. Khing: A beautifully illustrated book without text. We follow two dogs as they pursue two rats that have stolen their cake. Many feelings to identify and track

This Is Not My Hat by Jon Klassen: Stealing a hat from a large fish isn't always a good idea. The big fish will have feelings about it!

All for Me and None for All by Helen Lester: Wanting everything for himself gives those around Gruntly the pig lots of feelings!

Something Might Happen by Helen Lester: Poor Twitchly has many worries, but his Aunt Bridget wants to help him feel better.

Hamlet and the Enormous Chinese Dragon Kit by Brian Lies: Quince, a porcupine who worries, and his best friend Hamlet, a pig who loves taking risks, pair up in an adventure.

Hamlet and the Magnificent Sandcastle by Brian Lies: Hamlet and Quince again embark on an adventure with many feelings. Great for contrasting character feelings and talking about worries.

Hedgehog Bakes a Cake by Maryann Macdonald: Hedgehog's friends want to help bake a cake but their efforts only make him frustrated. Not to worry, it all works out in the end.

Katie and the Dinosaurs by James Mayhew: Beautifully illustrated story about Katie's adventures in a museum. Lots of different feelings, loved by any child who likes dinosaurs.

Enemy Pie by Derek Munson: What can you do when your only enemy moves in next door to your friend? Make Enemy Pie of course!

Bug Makes a Splash! (Kimochis) by Amy Novesky: Kimochis™ character Bug struggles to overcome his fears.

Cat's Not-So-Perfect Sandcastle (Kimochis) by Amy Novesky: Kimochis™ character Cat struggles with inflexibility and frustration.

Cloud's Best Worst Day Ever (Kimochis) by Amy Novesky: Kimochis™ character Cloud works hard to turn a bad day around.

Beatrice Doesn't Want To by Laura Numeroff: Beatrice doesn't like books or the library, but there she is with her brother Henry. It's frustrating for Henry until he finds a solution!

Piggie Pie! by Margie Palatini: Super story about a witch who will not stop to get pigs to make into pie. In addition to feelings, great for working on perspective taking.

Sam's Sandwich by David Pelham: A classic for perspective taking, deceit, and of course, feelings.

Dragon Gets By (series) by Dav Pilkey: Dragon often takes things literally and gets confused. Very nice illustrations of feelings in these chapter books.

Curious George Rides a Bike (series) by H.A. Rey: Curious George is always having adventures that somehow end up including lots of comfortable and uncomfortable feelings.

Who Will Tuck Me in Tonight? by Carol Roth: Lovely story about a lamb missing his mother at bedtime and the array of animals who try to help in their own way. Very good for talking about worries and building frustration.

Dragon Loves Tacos by Adam Rubin: Dragons love tacos but not the spicy salsa. A good book for basic work on feelings.

Those Darn Squirrels! by Adam Rubin: Follow the conflict between Old Man Bookwire and the squirrels plotting to get to his birdfeeders.

Mr. Putter and Tabby (series) by Cynthia Rylant: Series that follows Mr. Putter, his cat Tabby, his neighbor Mrs. Teaberry, and her dog Zeke through many adventures.

Ladybug Girl and Bumblebee Boy by David Soman and Jacky Davis: Lulu and her friend Sam try to work out what to do during recess. Nice illustrations and lots of basic emotions to talk about.

Caps for Sale by Esphyr Slobodkina: A great classic story to follow angry feelings that get bigger and bigger.

Sylvester and the Magic Pebble by William Steig: Caldecott winner full of emotions. It never gets old.

A Camping Spree with Mr. Magee by Chris Van Dusen: Mr. Magee and his dog Dee look forward to a peaceful camping trip. All is well until a bear shows up!

The Circus Ship by Chris Van Dusen: A town helps circus animals hide from the mean circus owner Mr. Paine. Bright, lovely illustrations of feelings.

Randy Riley's Really Big Hit by Chris Van Dusen: Randy Riley isn't good at baseball, but he can still save a town from disaster. Lots of feelings to discuss in this super book!

Amanda & Her Alligator! by Mo Willems: Amanda and Alligator are great friends, but even friends sometimes have uncomfortable feelings about each other. A chapter picture book by a fabulous author and illustrator.

Elephant and Piggie (series) by Mo Willems: Good friends Gerald and Piggie are always thinking about each other. And having lots of feelings. Classic simple books with nicely illustrated emotions.

The Quarreling Book by Charlotte Zolotow: Great story about how bad feelings can be contagious.

Appendix C

Visual Supports for Emotional Development

You may want to check out these resources to support emotional learning:

Kimochis™— These loveable characters can be used as a playful way to help children learn to identify and express feelings. Plush characters, storybooks, individual feelings realized on small plush circles, online materials. www.kimochis.com

EmotiPlush™ Toys—These wonderful dolls with moveable facial features (mouth, eyebrows) allow children to be shown and themselves demonstrate changing feelings. Plush dolls, storybooks. www.emoti-plush.com

Basic Four Emotions — Pictorial

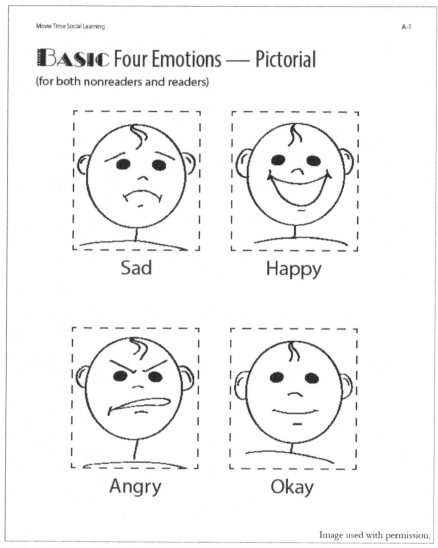

Expanded Six Emotions — Pictorial

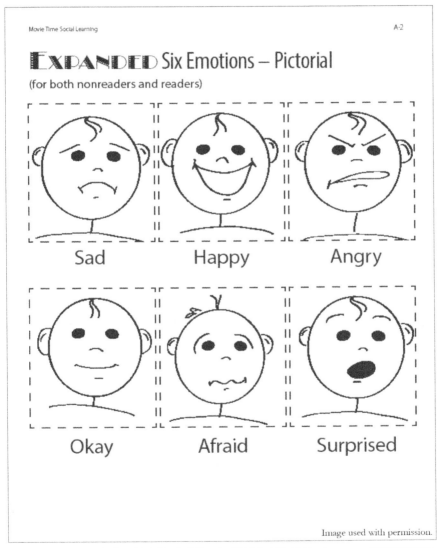

Intermediate Feelings List

Afraid	Angry	Happy	Sad	Surprised
afraid	angry	cheerful	disappointed	blown away
anxious	annoyed	encouraged	lonely	shocked
cautious	bothered	fine	sad	surprised
frantic	cranky	glad	unhappy	
freaked out	explosive	grateful	upset	
frightened	frustrated	happy		
jumpy	furious	proud		
nervous	grouchy			**Excited**
panicked	grumpy			excited
scared	irritated			
stressed	mad			
terrified				
threatened				
worried				
Interested	**Hurt**	**Sorry**	**Unsure**	**Sure**
interested	hated	embarrassed	clueless	brave
	hurt	sorry	confused	certain
	ignored	stupid	shy	competitive
			unsure	confident
				sure
Sneaky	**Liked**	**Okay**	**Unfriendly**	**Wanting**
mischievous	accepted	calm	bossy	greedy
sneaky	included	okay	hateful	hopeful
	liked		mean	jealous
	needed		rude	wanting
			unfriendly	

Feelings Lists are adapted from the following:

Baron-Cohen, S. (2007). *Mind reading: The interactive guide to emotions* (v.1.3) [CD-ROM]. London, England: Jessica Kingsley Publishers.

Baron-Cohen, S., Golan, O., Wheelwright, S., Granader, Y., & Hill, J. (2010). Emotion word comprehension from 4 to 16 years old: A developmental survey. *Frontiers in Evolutionary Neuroscience, 2,* 109.

Ekman, P. (2007). *Emotions revealed: Recognizing faces and feelings to improve communication and emotional life* (2nd ed.). New York, NY: Henry Holt and Company, LLC.

McAfee, J. (2002). *Navigating the social world.* Arlington, TX: Future Horizons, Inc.

Advanced Feelings List

Afraid	Angry	Happy	Sad	Surprised
afraid	angry	amused	depressed	amazed
alarmed	annoyed	cheerful	despairing	appalled
anxious	bitter	delighted	devastated	astonished
cautious	bothered	ecstatic	disappointed	blown away
cowardly	complaining	encouraged	discouraged	dismayed
desperate	cranky	fine	dissatisfied	horrified
disturbed	displeased	glad	gloomy	shocked
dreading	enraged	happy	heartbroken	startled
frantic	exasperated	grateful	hopeless	surprised
freaked out	explosive	overjoyed	lonely	
frightened	frustrated	proud	lost	
intimidated	furious	triumphant	miserable	
jumpy	grouchy		mistreated	
nervous	grumpy		misunderstood	
overwhelmed	impatient		resigned	
panicked	indignant		sad	
scared	infuriated		troubled	
stressed	irritated		unhappy	
terrified	mad		upset	
threatened	outraged		withdrawn	
trapped	provoked			
vulnerable	wild			
worried				
Disgusted	**Disbelieving**	**Kind**	**Bored**	**Excited**
disgusted	cautious	comforting	bored	alert
grossed out	disbelieving	concerned	distant	eager
revolted	doubtful	encouraging	distracted	enthusiastic
	suspicious	forgiving	indifferent	excited
		friendly	unenthusiastic	silly
		helpful	unimpressed	thrilled
		kind		
		patient understanding		

Interested	Hurt	Shamed	Unsure	Sure
curious	abused	ashamed	ambivalent	arrogant
fascinated	attacked	embarrassed	bashful	bossy
focused	betrayed	disgraced	bewildered	brave
impatient	blamed	foolish	clueless	certain
impressed	bullied	guilty	confused	cocky
interested	cheated	humiliated	defeated	competitive
tempted	criticized	shamed	doubtful	confident
	disliked	sorry	hesitant	courageous
	disrespected	stupid	insecure	determined
	hated		puzzled	prepared
	hurt		reluctant	pushy
	ignored		self-conscious	smug
	insulted		shy	strong
	neglected		uncertain	stubborn
	offended		uncomfortable	sure
	patronized		unsure	
Sneaky	**Liked**	**Okay**	**Unfriendly**	**Wanting**
devious	accepted	calm	aggressive	begging
mischievous	appreciated	content	argumentative	demanding
mysterious	comforted	indifferent	contemptuous	greedy
sneaky	forgiven	okay	cruel	hopeful
	included	satisfied	defensive	jealous
	liked		defiant	needy wanting
	needed		disagreeable	wishful
	praised		disapproving	
	supported		disrespectful	
	welcomed		hateful	
			judgmental	
			mean	
			rejecting	
			rude	
			sarcastic	
			selfish	
			threatening	
			unfriendly	
			unkind	

Feelings Lists are adapted from the following:

Baron-Cohen, S. (2007). *Mind reading: The interactive guide to emotions* (v.1.3) [CD-ROM]. London, England: Jessica Kingsley Publishers.

Baron-Cohen, S., Golan, O., Wheelwright, S., Granader, Y., & Hill, J. (2010). Emotion word comprehension from 4 to 16 years old: A developmental survey. *Frontiers in Evolutionary Neuroscience, 2*, 109.

Ekman, P. (2007). *Emotions revealed: Recognizing faces and feelings to improve communication and emotional life* (2nd ed.). New York, NY: Henry Holt and Company LLC.

McAfee, J. (2002). *Navigating the social world*. Arlington, TX: Future Horizons, Inc.

Appendix D

List of Interjections

Note: Many of these interjections can be used to communicate empathy, reflecting an understanding of comfortable as well as uncomfortable feelings based on intonation. For example, "eww" could mean "great" in response to "I got a new computer for my birthday!" or "too bad" in response to "I cracked the screen on my phone today." Interjections provide a great opportunity to work on expression. Be sure to add whatever interjections are popular in your community.

• Aha • Ahh • Alright • Argh • Awful • Awww	• Boo • Boy • Bummer • Come on • Cool	• Darn • Drat • Duh • Eek • Eh • Eww	• Gee • Gee whiz • Good • Good grief • Good job • Gosh • Great • Grrrrh	• Ha • Ha-ha • Hmm • Holy cow • Hooray • Huh • Ich • Jeez
• Man • Meh • Mhmm • Mmmmm • My word	• Nah • Nice • No • Now • No way • Nuh-uh • Nuts	• Oh • Oh dear • Oh my • Oh no • Oh well • Okay • Oo-la-la • Oops • Ouch • Ow • Oy	• Pee-you • Phew • Please • Rats • Right • Right on	• Sheesh • Shoot • Shucks • Sorry • That sucks • Too bad • Tsk • Tut-tut
• Ugh • Uh • Uh-huh • Uh-Oh • Um	• Waa • What • Whatever • Whoa • Whoops • Wow	• Ya • Yay • Yeah • Yes • Yikes • Yuck • Yum		

Appendix E

Sample Parent Information Letterhead

Your letterhead here

Date

Dear _____,

In my work with your child this year, I will be using a new therapy program called YouCue Feelings: Using Online Videos for Social Learning (Vagin, 2015). This program uses structured viewing of pre-selected YouTube videos to teach children important social thinking concepts. YouCue Feelings focuses on (1) expanding your child's feelings vocabulary, (2) improving his or her overall ability to track changes in feelings over time, and (3) supporting your child's ability to talk about his or her own feelings (especially uncomfortable feelings, like "sad," "mad," and "scared"). We will start by focusing on characters in videos, and then encourage your child to talk about his or her own experiences.

Attached you will find a release form. Please fill it out and return it with your child as soon as possible. Be assured that the YouTube videos your child will be viewing will be age appropriate and used within the context of an interactive therapeutic program and that they will not be seeing YouTube commercials (these are often not child appropriate). Please feel free to call me with any questions or comments.

Thanks so much!

Your name here

Bibliography

Baron-Cohen, S. (1995). *Mindblindness*: An essay on autism and theory of mind. Cambridge, MA: MIT Press.

Baron-Cohen, S. (2007). *Mind reading: The interactive guide to emotions* (v.1.3) [CD-ROM], London, England: Jessica Kingsley Publishers.

Baron-Cohen, S., Golan, O., Wheelwright, S., Granader, Y., & Hill, J. (2010). Emotion word comprehension from 4 to 16 years old: A developmental survey. *Frontiers in Evolutionary Neuroscience*, 2, 109.

Bloom, L. (1998). Language development and emotional expression. *Pediatrics*, 102 (5), 1272–1277.

Barrett, L. F., Gross, J., Christensen, T. C., & Benvenuto, M. (2001). Knowing what you're feeling and knowing what to do about it: Mapping the relation between emotion differentiation and emotional regulation. *Cognition and Emotion*, 15 (6), 713–724.

Dunn Buron, K. & Curtis, M. (2012). *The incredible 5-point scale, The significantly improved and expanded second edition*. Shawnee Mission, KS: AAPC Publishing.

Ekman, P. (2007). *Emotions revealed: Recognizing faces and feelings to improve communication and emotional life* (2nd ed.). New York, NY: Henry Holt and Company LLC.

Goleman, D. (2005). *Emotional Intelligence: Why it can matter more than IQ*. New York, NY: Bantam Books.

Kaiser, M. D. & Pelphrey, K. A. (2012). Disrupted action perception in autism: Behavioral evidence, neuroendophenotypes, and diagnostic utility. *Developmental Cognitive Neuroscience*, 2, 25–35.

Kahneman, D. (2011). *Thinking, fast and slow*. New York, NY: Farrar, Straus and Giroux.

Klin, A., Lin, D., Gorrindo, P., Ramsay, G., & Jones, W. (2009). Two-year-olds with autism orient to nonsocial contingencies rather than biological motion. *Nature*, 459, 257–261.

Kroeger, A., Bletsch, A., Krick, C., Siniatchkin, S., Jarczok, J., Freitag, C., & Bender, S. (2013). Visual event-related potentials to biological motion stimuli in autism spectrum disorders. *Social Cognitive and Affective Neuroscience Advance Access*, Aug. 19, 1–9.

Kuypers, L. (2011). *The zones of regulation*. San Jose, CA: Think Social Publishing, Inc.

Lipton, M. E. & Nowicki, S. (2009). The social-emotional learning framework (SELF): A guide for understanding brain-based social-emotional learning impairments. *The Journal of Developmental Processes*, 4(2), 99–115.

McAfee, J. (2002). *Navigating the social world*. Arlington, TX: Future Horizons, Inc.

Suskind, R. (2014). *Life, animated: a story of sidekicks, heroes, and autism*. New York, NY: Kingswell.

Tomkins, S. S. (2008). *Affect Imagery Consciousness*. New York, NY: Springer Publishing Company.

Ukrainetz, T. A. (1998). Beyond Vygotsky: What Soviet activity theory offers naturalistic language intervention. *Journal of Speech-Language Pathology and Audiology*, 22(3), 164–175.

Vagin, A. (2012). *Movie time social learning*. San Jose, CA: Think Social Publishing, Inc.

Vermeulen, P. (2012). *Autism as context blindness*. Shawnee Mission, KS: AAPC Publishing.

Winner, M. G. (2005). *Think social! A social thinking curriculum for school-age students*. San Jose, CA: Think Social Publishing, Inc.

Made in the USA
Monee, IL
17 September 2020